Loen Unicorn

Check out these other

Uden Unicorn

books!

Uden Unicorn's Playdate

Uden Unicorn and the Royal Butterfly

Coming soon!

Uden Unicorn and the Runaway Rollercoaster

Writer and Illustrator: Jason Wilburn
Editor and Activities Writer: Tamara Wilburn
Photo and Illustration Contributor: Tucker Wilburn

First American Edition 2023
Second American Edition 2024

www.udenunicorn.com
ISBN: 9798338057575

Uden Unicorn's

Bottles, Boxes, and Bags

To my family.
Without your support, I never could have followed this dream.

Table of Contents

Jolly Jester is spending a few hours at Uden's house after school. Jolly and Uden are classmates, but they're not close friends. Their moms are friends.

"We need to stop at the **store**," explains Mom. "Then we can go home for a **snack**."

"What can we have for a snack?" asks Uden.

"Let's let our **guest** choose," says Mom.

"**Donuts**!" shouts Jolly.

"Donuts are my **favorite** ," explains Jolly.

Uden doesn't eat donuts often, but he likes them. Today's snack might be a **rare** treat.

"Your mom says that's OK. We can get donuts," **announces** Mom.

Uden and Jolly are very excited. Mom adds "donuts" to the bottom of the **shopping list** .

"Can you two **guide** our shopping trip?" Mom asks. She hands the shopping list to Jolly.

Uden likes helping to find the **items** in the store. But Uden is worried.

Stop and Think
Selecting a Snack

Uden doesn't eat donuts often. Usually, he has fruits or vegetables for a snack. But why? Why doesn't Uden eat donuts all the time?

Food is important. It gives our bodies **calories**. We need calories to run and play, or even just to breathe. We need calories to live.

However, too many calories can be a problem. Our bodies store extra calories as fat. Fat can keep you alive when there's no food. But too much fat can cause health problems.

It's OK to have a treat every now and then, but think about what you eat. Make the food choices that are right for your body. Stay healthy!

Activities (for pages 6-11)

A. Choose and write.

announces	store	rare	item	favorite	guest	donut	guide
shopping list	snack						

1. We go to the ________ to get food.
2. The ________ has icing and a hole in the middle.
3. I can't find the last ________ I need to make breakfast.
4. She has a ________ after school.
5. Molly is our ________ for the weekend.
6. He will ________ us around the museum.
7. Let's make a ________ so we know what to buy.
8. The teacher ________ the winner of the contest.
9. What is your ________ dessert?
10. They discovered a ________ stone.

B. Circle T (True) or F (False).

1. Jolly and Uden are best friends. T / F
2. Jolly would like donuts for a snack. T / F
3. Mom puts milk on the shopping list. T / F
4. Uden enjoys helping his mom at the store. T / F
5. Uden is excited to guide the shopping trip with Jolly. T / F

C. Read and write.

ask Jolly's mom	guide their trip	before going home
ready to begin shopping	allows Jolly to pick	

Uden, Jolly, and Uden's mom need to stop at the store
1. ______________________. Before starting, Mrs. Unicorn
2. ______________________ the snack they will get. Donuts! She has to
3. ______________________ if he can have them. She says, "OK." Now
they are 4. ______________________. Uden and Jolly will
5. ______________________ today.

D. Circle the correct answers.

1. What does Uden normally eat for a snack?
a. donuts and muffins b. fruits and vegetables c. meat and potatoes
2. How do we get calories?
a. running b. breathing c. eating
3. Where do our bodies store extra calories?
a. fat b. food c. snacks
4. How often should you eat snacks?
a. all the time b. never c. sometimes

Jolly likes to make **jokes** . It's hard to do schoolwork when Jolly is your **partner** .

Would he be a good partner for guiding the shopping trip?

"What's the first item on our list?" asks Mom.

"A **bottle** of **jelly**," says Jolly.

Uden stares at Jolly. Did Jolly say a "bottle" of jelly? Jelly doesn't come in a bottle.

"A '**jar**' of jelly I think," smiles Mom.

Jolly smiles too. He likes that Mom is **playing along** .

"A jar is like a bottle," thinks Uden. Uden thinks Jolly must have made a mistake.

"What's **next**?" Mom asks.

"A jar of **rice**," says Jolly.

Uden thinks. What is Jolly saying? Jelly comes in a jar, but rice doesn't.

"No!" says Uden. "Not a 'jar' of rice. Rice comes in a **bag**!"

"Yes," says Mom. "We'll get a bag of rice. But it's ok, Uden. Jolly is just having fun."

Uden **frowns**. He doesn't think this is fun.

Stop and Think

Working With Others

Everyone is different. Some people are quiet and reserved. Others are loud and boisterous. Usually, this difference can be celebrated. But sometimes, differences can make it hard to get along.

Be considerate of the people you're with. Are they loud and boisterous, or are they quiet and reserved? It might be polite to act more in the way they do while you're together.

It can be hard if someone is not being considerate of you. The way they act might make you upset. Sometimes it's easiest to remember that you won't be together long.

Of course, if someone is being rude, you can say something. Try your best not to yell or get angry. Work together to make your time together as rewarding as possible.

Activities (for pages 14-19)

A. Match.

1. Bag 2. Bottle 3. Jar 4. Jelly 5. Rice

B. Circle the correct answers.

1. Who likes to make jokes?
a. Uden b. Mom c. Jolly

2. Uden isn't sure Jolly will be a good ________.
a. partner b. shopper c. teacher

3. What does Jolly like about Mrs. Unicorn?
a. She takes him shopping. b. She plays along. c. She is buying donuts.

4. What is next on the list, after jelly?
a. rice b. donuts c. cereal

5. How do we know Uden isn't having fun?
a. He laughs. b. He smiles. c. He frowns.

C. Read and write.

bag	frown	rice	partners	jar	bottle

We will be ____________ for guiding the shopping trip. I think we need a ____________ of jelly!

I know Jolly means a ____________ of jelly. I'll play along with him. Uh oh, Jolly says the next item is a jar of ____________. Uden is getting upset.

I ____________ and tell Mom and Jolly that rice comes in a ____________!

D. Circle T (True) or F (False).

1. Everyone is the same. (T / F)

2. Differences can make it hard to get along. (T / F)

3. If you are considerate, you act more like the people you are with. (T / F)

4. It's easiest to remember that you will be together forever. (T / F)

5. You can say something if someone is being rude to you. (T / F)

"Next?" asks Mom.

"A **loaf** of milk," says Jolly.

This is **ridiculous** ! Who ever heard of a loaf of milk? Jolly is making mistakes on purpose.

"No Jolly! We need a **jug** of milk!" yells Uden.

Mom and Jolly frown.

"You **ruin** everything!" continues Uden. "This is why no one wants to be partners with you at school."

"Uden Unicorn!" says Mom, **sternly** . "Jolly is our guest, and he's just having fun."

"But he **always** does this. His fun ruins everything at school," cries Uden.

"This isn't school, Uden." says Mom. "We can have fun together at the store."

"But this isn't fun," insists Uden. "It's **frustrating** ."

"It's kind of fun," says Mom. "Can you **imagine** a loaf of milk?"

Uden giggles.

"I'm **sorry**," Jolly says. "I was just trying to make you laugh."

Uden feels bad. Jolly was just having fun.

"No. I'm sorry," says Uden. "It's ok to **joke around** sometimes."

Stop and Think

Group Work

Uden knows that working in groups can be hard. Getting many different minds to focus on one task is frustrating. Everyone wants to do their own thing.

Some people, like Jolly, would rather make jokes and play than work on a task. When the work is easy, Uden doesn't mind Jolly's jokes as much. It's when a task is hard, or when it's something Uden is very excited about that Jolly becomes hard to work with.

If you know someone like Jolly, try to understand them. Are they trying to make you laugh? If they are, thank them, but tell them you'd like to play later.

Also, sometimes people play and joke around when they're nervous. Maybe they don't know how to do the task. They may be too shy to ask for help. Offer to help them instead of playing.

Activities (for pages 20-27)

A. Match.

Ridiculous | Ruin | Sternly | Frustrating | Imagine | Joke around

B. Circle the correct answers.

1. What does Jolly say they need?
a) a loaf of bread b) a loaf of milk c) a jug of milk

2. What does Uden say Jolly always does at school?
a) ruins everything b) runs away c) studies hard

3. How does Uden feel after Jolly says, "I'm sorry"?
a) fun b) bad c) mad

C. Read and write.

ridiculous	sorry	ruins	loaf	imagine	frustrating	jug

Uden's mom asks for the next item. "A ____________ of milk!" I'm being ____________ and making mistakes on purpose.

I'm getting mad! "No, we need a ____________ of milk! I yell at Jolly. Jolly ____________ everything. Jolly is very ____________.

I need to talk to Uden. "Can you ____________ a loaf of milk?" The idea makes Uden giggle. Jolly and Uden both say they are ____________.

D. Circle the correct words.

1. Uden understands that working in groups can be (hard / easy).
2. Jolly would rather make jokes and (work / play) than be on task.
3. Jolly is just trying to make Uden (work / laugh).
4. It's a good idea to say you'd like to play (later / now).
5. People might joke around if they are (scared / nervous).
6. Offer to (focus / help) them instead of playing.

"So..." starts Mom slowly. "What's the next item on the list?" Jolly **hands** the list to Uden.

"Here, Uden," Jolly says, "you can guide the shopping trip."

"A **can** of cereal," says Uden.

Mom and Jolly smile. It's much nicer when everyone plays together.

"I think you mean a **box** of cereal," replies Jolly.

Mom helps them choose a **healthy** cereal.

"We need a box of ketchup next," says Jolly.

Uden imagines a box of ketchup. **Yuck**!

The ketchup would **leak** through the box.

"I think we should get a bottle of ketchup instead," says Uden. "The **glass** bottle will hold the ketchup better."

Uden adds the bottle of ketchup to the **cart**.

"Now we need **bread**," says Uden.

"Yes," agrees Jolly. "We need a **carton** of bread."

Uden starts to laugh.

Bread is soft. A carton would squish the bread. It would be silly to put bread in a carton.

Stop and Think

Going Along to Get Along

Uden likes to do things his way. He really doesn't like change. Sometimes this causes Uden problems. But he has learned a trick to get along.

Often, it's easier to participate in an activity than to resist. While you should never do anything you're uncomfortable doing, trying new things with people is a great way to become friends. Sharing new experiences helps people bond.

It's good to want to do things your own way. You know what works for you. You know how to do it that way. But it's also important to get along with others. Flexibility allows you to experience things from another perspective. Maybe you'll learn a way of doing something that you prefer.

Activities (for pages 30-35)

A. Look and match.

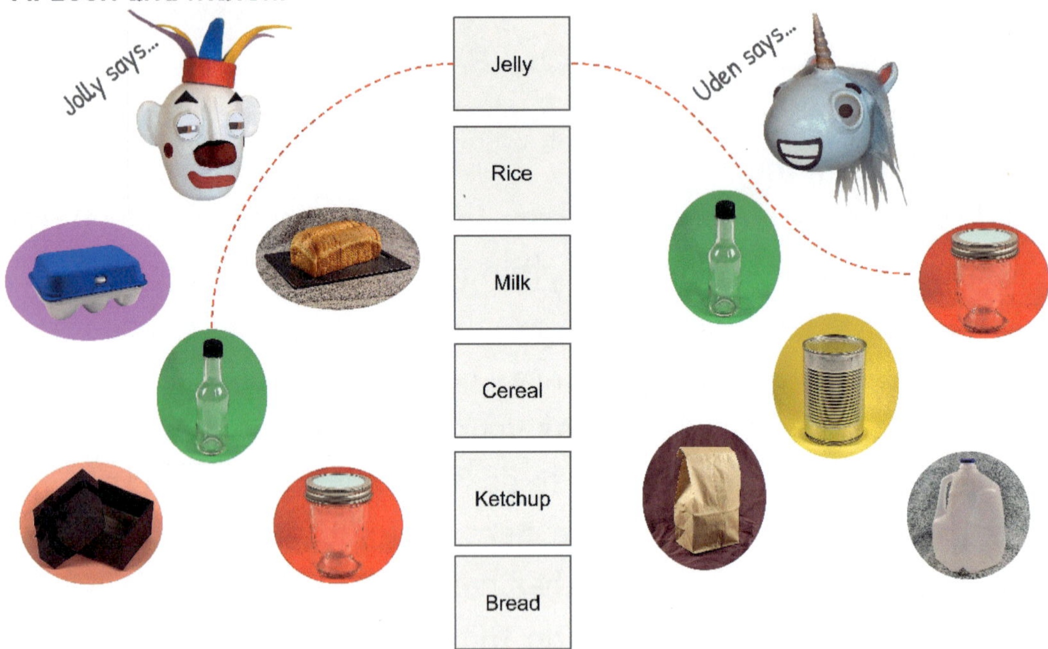

B. Circle the correct words.

1. Jolly hands the (shopping list / shopping cart) to Uden.
2. Uden surprised Mom and Jolly when he (plays along / laughs out loud) with them.
3. Mom helps Uden and Jolly choose a healthy (bag of eggs / box of cereal).
4. Uden thinks, "yuck!" because a (jar of flowers / box of ketchup) would leak.
5. Uden puts a (glass bottle / paper bag) of ketchup in the cart.
6. Jolly makes Uden laugh when he says that they need a (carton of bread / carton of eggs).

C. Read and write.

plays along with them	bread next	of ketchup in the cart	healthy box of cereal
a box of ketchup would leak	hands the shopping list to Uden		

Jolly 1. ______________________. Uden surprised Mom and Jolly when he 2. ______________________. Mom helps Uden and Jolly choose a 3. ______________________. Uden thinks, "yuck!" because 4. ______________________ though the box. Uden puts a glass bottle 5. ______________________. Uden reads the next item on the list. They need 6. ____________. Jolly makes Uden laugh when he says that they need a carton of bread.

D. Write the sentences in the correct order.

1. (change. / Uden / doesn't like / really)

____

2. (is a great / become friends. / Trying / new things with / way to / people)

____

3. (your own / It's / to do / way. / good to want / things)

____

4. (to experience / another perspective. / allows you / things / Flexibility / from)

____

"I'll get a loaf of bread this time," smiles Mom.

She takes a loaf of bread and places it **on top** of the other **groceries** .

"What's next?" sighs Mom **playfully** .

Jolly hands the list to Uden again.

"A jug of **peas**," laughs Uden.

A jug would hold the peas well, but a jug is really big.

"I don't think we could eat a **whole** jug of peas," laughs Mom.

"You'd better get a can of peas then," laughs Jolly. Jolly **adds** the can of peas to the cart.

"OK, Jolly," sighs Mom, "What's next?"

"A bag of eggs!" Jolly says.

"Oh no!" says Uden, imagining a bag of eggs. "That wouldn't work at all!"

Eggs are **delicate** . They need a special **container** .

"I'll get some eggs packed safely in a carton," smiles Mom.

She places the eggs **carefully** in the cart. She doesn't want them to get **crushed** .

Stop and Think

Managing Mischief

When a friend is misbehaving, you need to make a choice. You can join your friend. You can watch and do nothing. You can tell an adult. Or, you could try to **convince** your friend to behave differently.

First, ask yourself if what your friend is doing is dangerous. If it is, tell an adult at once. Friends don't like it when they get in trouble, but that's better than getting hurt.

If your friend isn't doing anything dangerous, ask yourself what rule they are breaking. Will they get in trouble for what they are doing? Say something to your friend. Ask them to behave differently.

Peers influence each other. They can be a good influence or a bad one. Try your best to be a good influence.

Activities (for pages 38-43)

A. Choose and write.

crushed	groceries	on top	peas	whole

1. Meg and I took the ____________ out of the car.
2. There as a large owl ____________ of the light pole.
3. She doesn't really like to have ____________ with dinner.
4. Dave can eat a ____________ pizza by himself.
5. Oh no! The cookies got ____________ by the heavy watermelon.

B. Circle true (T) or false (F).

1. They decide to get a loaf of milk. (T / F)
2. The groceries are on top of the bread. (T / F)
3. Jolly says that they should get a jug of peas. (T / F)
4. Mom doesn't think they can eat a whole jug of peas. (T / F)
5. A can of peas is delicate. (T / F)
6. Eggs come in a bag. (T / F)
7. Mom places the eggs carefully in the cart. (T / F)
8. The eggs get crushed. (T / F)

C. Read and write.

playfully delicate crushed carefully container groceries

I put the loaf of bread into the cart with the other ____________. Then I ____________ ask, "what's next?"

Jolly suggested a bag of eggs. But I know that eggs are ____________. They need to be in a special ____________.

I have to put the eggs into the cart ____________. This way, they won't get ____________.

D. Choose and write.

convince choose misbehaving adult nothing

1. My friend is ____________.

2. You can ____________ to join me, or watch and say ____________.

3. Or, I can tell an ____________. I might try to ____________ Jolly to change the way he is behaving.

"The next thing on the list is a **bucket** of flowers," says Jolly.

Uden sees the large bucket of flowers. He giggles. Mom doesn't **need** that many flowers.

"I think I'll just get one **bouquet** today," smiles Mom. She chooses a purple bouquet that **matches** her eyes.

"What else do we need?" asks Mom.

"We need a bag of donuts," says Jolly.

"He **means** a box of donuts," **corrects** Uden.

"**Nope**!" says Jolly happily. "I mean a bag of donuts."

"Oh!" says Uden in surprise. He didn't **realize** that donuts could come in a bag.

"These are my favorite donuts. They come in a bag," explains Jolly. "I hope you **enjoy** them as much as I do, **friend**."

And Uden thought they were the most delicious donuts ever.

Stop and Think
A Shared Snack

Sharing food is a special way to share oneself. It helps us bond with the people around us. You might think that everyone eats the same food, but you'll be surprised.

Every family enjoys different food. Maybe, it's grandma's secret cake recipe. Perhaps, it's a barbecue recipe Dad found on the Internet. Or maybe it's not the recipe, but simply the way Mom makes her enchilada casserole. Your family's meals are unique.

Think about the things your friends like to eat. Is there something your family eats that they would enjoy? Maybe you can invite your friends to dinner or bring something to share at lunch. Sharing a meal is a great way to bring you closer together.

Activities (for pages 46-51)

A. Choose and write.

bucket	need	bouquet	matches
mean	correct	realize	friends

1. The color of the sky ____________ her eyes.
2. She had to ____________ the mistake she made.
3. We don't really ____________ any more pets.
4. The boys are good ____________ now.
5. He gave the horse a ____________ of water to drink.
6. What I ____________ is, I will be a little late.
7. Dad gave Mom a ____________ of flowers.
8. They didn't ____________ that it had started to rain.

B. Who says this? Read and match.

1.  • • "I think I'll just get one bouquet today."

2.  • • "He means a box of donuts."

3.  • • "These are my favorite donuts. They come in a bag. I hope you enjoy them as much as I do, friend."

C. Choose and write.

bucket	donuts	nope	bouquet	purple	corrects

I want to get some ___________ flowers to match my eyes. I will just get a ___________ of flowers. I don't need a ___________ of them.

It's time for ___________! When I say we need a bag of donuts, Uden ___________ me. But I say, "___________!" because the donuts really do come in a bag, not a box.

D. Circle the correct words.

1. Sharing food helps us (realize / bond) with the people around us.
2. Not everyone eats the same (food / flowers).
3. Each family's meals are (playful / unique).
4. Your mom's (flower / enchilada) casserole might be a unique food for your family.
5. Consider the (special / careful) things your friends like.
6. (Sharing / Needing) a meal with friends can bring us closer.

Fun and Games

Uden's Crazy Story

For each of the numbers below, write words of your choosing for each part of speech. Read your words when you see the matching numbers in the story. Some word forms will change slightly. (You'll see.)

You can make many different stories by changing the words again and again!

1. place	4. job	7. container	10. emotion	13. container
2. food	5. verb	8. food	11. verb	14. food
3. noun	6. verb	9. verb	12. verb	15. container

Uden and Jolly are going to the 1.. They will get 2. for a snack. Mom gives the 3. to Jolly. Uden feels worried.

Uden doesn't think Jolly will make a good 4.. Jolly likes to 5.. Uden likes to 6..

Jolly says to get a 7. of jelly. Then, he says to get a jar of 8.. How ridiculous!

Jolly and Uden 9.. Everyone is 10.. Then, Uden decides to 11..

Now, Uden and Jolly have fun 12.. They get a 13. of cereal. They get a bottle of 14.. They get a 15. of eggs. Finally, they get a bag of 2.. Jolly and Uden eat their 2.. What a delicious snack!

SECRET MESSAGE SCRAMBLE

Unscramble the words and write them in the boxes. Use the clues if needed.

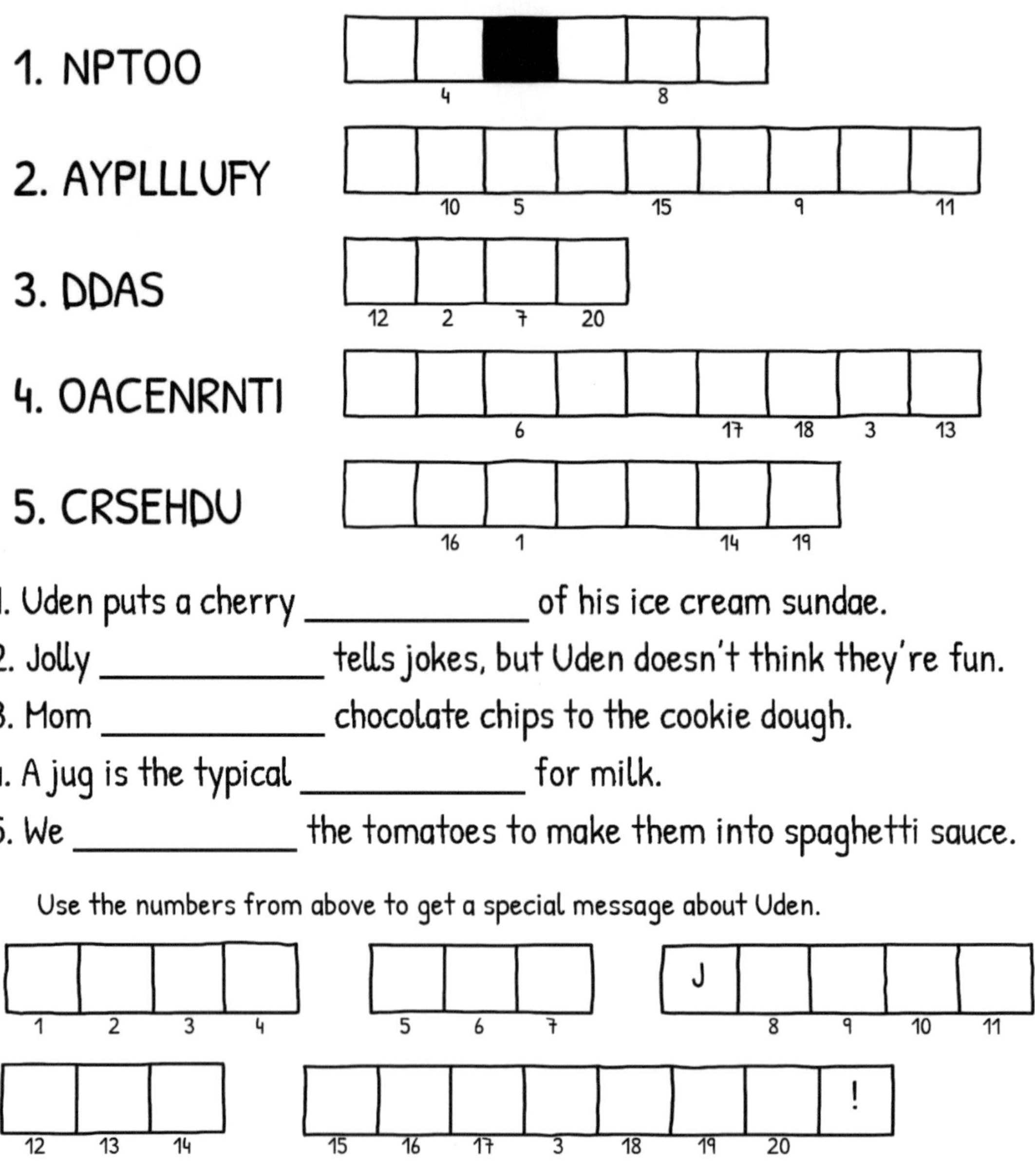

1. Uden puts a cherry ____________ of his ice cream sundae.
2. Jolly ____________ tells jokes, but Uden doesn't think they're fun.
3. Mom ____________ chocolate chips to the cookie dough.
4. A jug is the typical ____________ for milk.
5. We ____________ the tomatoes to make them into spaghetti sauce.

Use the numbers from above to get a special message about Uden.

Stars and Boxes

Take turns drawing a line between two stars. If your line makes a box, mark the box with your initial and go again. Count who has the most boxes at the end.

HANGMAN

Look through the glossary to chose a word. Draw blanks for each letter. Then, challenge a partner to guess the letters in your word. Beware! For each wrong letter, add a head, body arm or leg.

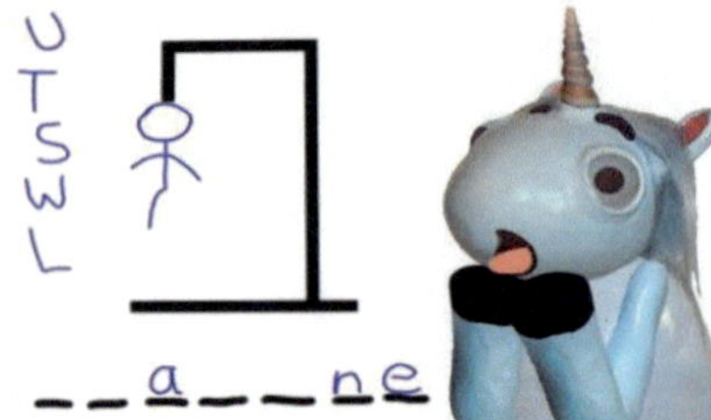

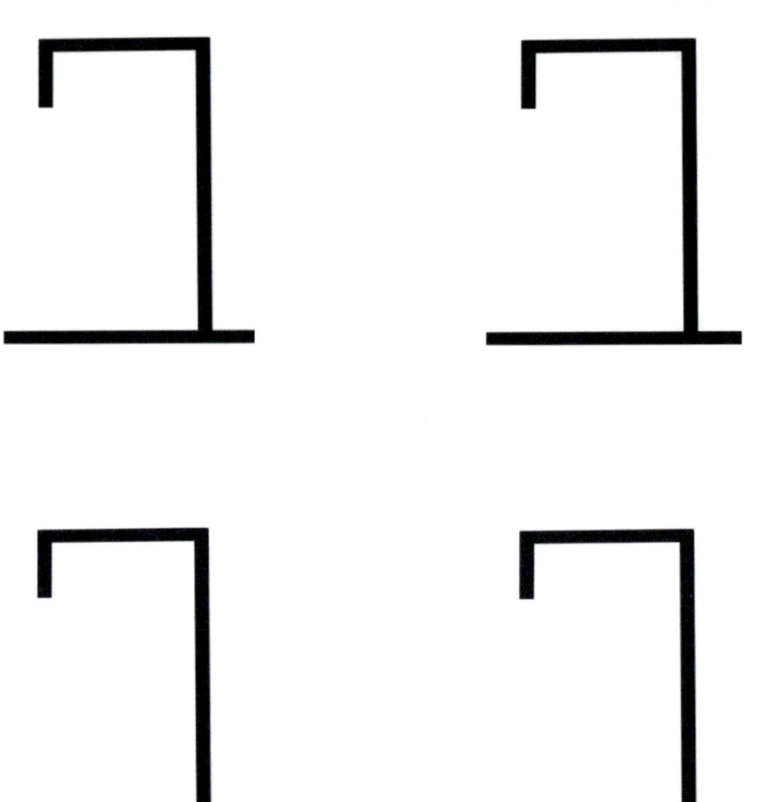

Wordsearch

Find the words in the box below hidden amoung the letters.

store	shopping list	jokes
frowns	ridiculous	imagine
healthy	bread	playfully
delicate	bucket	playdate

		e	f	s	n	b	p	s	o	r
		j	i	r	t	i	e	h	c	i
		o	d	s	o	o	s	o	k	t
		k	e	h	e	b	r	e	a	d
l	s	e	l	o	l	a	y	e	y	p
o	a	s	c	p	b	i	w	l	d	p
u	f	e	i	p	u	l	p	t	a	m
c	r	i	d	i	c	u	l	o	u	s
t	o	i	i	n	k	f	a	y	n	g
h	w	n	s	g	e	d	y	a	i	d
y	n	g	l	l	t	a	f	r	m	e
l	s	t	o	i	y	k	u	j	a	l
a	u	c	k	s	f	t	l	o	g	i
h	e	a	l	t	h	y	l	e	i	c
p	l	a	y	f	b	u	y	h	n	a
y	l	p	l	a	y	d	a	t	e	t
t	s	a	d	m	u	a	r	l	l	e

Tic Tac Toe

Take turns drawing an X or an O in one of the nine spaces. Try to get three of your mark in a row. Or, just try to stop your partner from getting three of their mark in a row. Draw a line through your three!

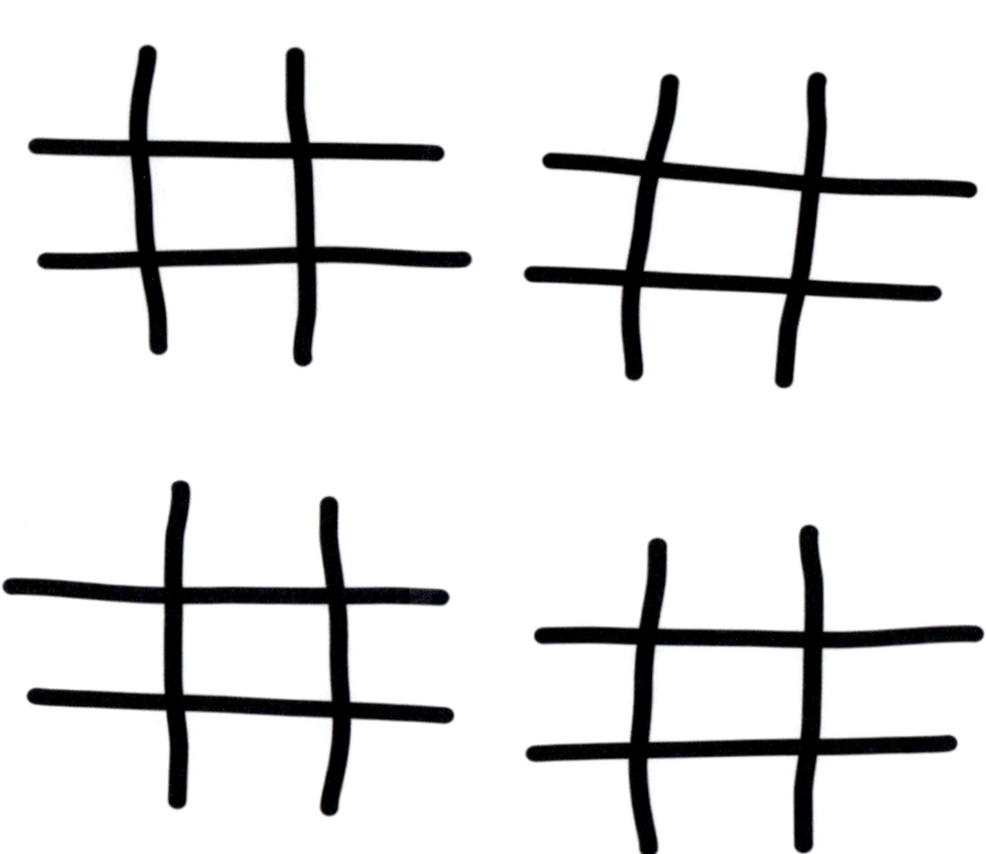

Answer Keys

Activities (AK) (for pages 6-11)

A. Choose and write.

announces store rare item favorite guest donut guide shopping list snack

1. We go to the store to get food.
2. The donut has icing and a hole in the middle.
3. I can't find the last item I need to make breakfast.
4. She has a snack after school.
5. Molly is our guest for the weekend.
6. He will guide us around the museum.
7. Let's make a shopping list so we know what to buy.
8. The teacher announces the winner of the contest.
9. What is your favorite dessert?
10. They discovered a rare stone.

B. Circle T (True) or F (False).

1. Jolly and Uden are best friends. T / (F)
2. Jolly would like donuts for a snack. (T) / F
3. Mom puts milk on the shopping list. T / (F)
4. Uden enjoys helping his mom at the store. (T) / F
5. Uden is excited to guide the shopping trip with Jolly. T / (F)

C. Read and write.

ask Jolly's mom guide their trip before going home ready to begin shopping allows Jolly to pick

Uden, Jolly, and Uden's mom need to stop at the store 1. before going home. Before starting, Mrs. Unicorn 2. allows Jolly to pick the snack they will get. Donuts! She has to 3. ask Jolly's mom if he can have them. She says, "OK." Now they are 4. ready to begin shopping. Uden and Jolly will 5. guide their trip today.

D. Circle the correct answers.

1. What does Uden normally eat for a snack?
a. donuts and muffins (b.) fruits and vegetables c. meat and potatoes

2. How do we get calories?
a. running b. breathing (c.) eating

3. Where do our bodies store extra calories?
(a.) fat b. food c. snacks

4. How often should you eat snacks?
a. all the time b. never (c.) sometimes

Activities (AK) (for pages 14-19)

A. Match.

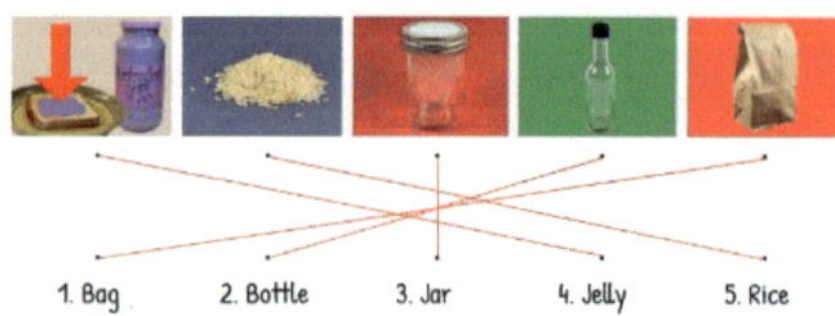

B. Circle the correct answers.

1. Who likes to make jokes?
a. Uden b. Mom (c.) Jolly

2. Uden isn't sure Jolly will be a good ________.
(a.) partner b. shopper c. teacher

3. What does Jolly like about Mrs. Unicorn?
a. She takes him shopping. (b.) She plays along. c. She is buying donuts.

4. What is next on the list, after jelly?
(a.) rice b. donuts c. cereal

5. How do we know Uden isn't having fun?
a. He laughs. b. He smiles. (c.) He frowns.

C. Read and write.

bag	frown	rice	partners	jar	bottle

D. Circle T (True) or F (False).

1. Everyone is the same. (T / (F))
2. Differences can make it hard to get along. ((T) / F)
3. If you are considerate, you act more like the people you are with. ((T) / F)
4. It's easiest to remember that you will be together forever. (T / (F))
5. You can say something if someone is being rude to you. ((T) / F)

Activities (AK) (for pages 22-27)

A. Match.

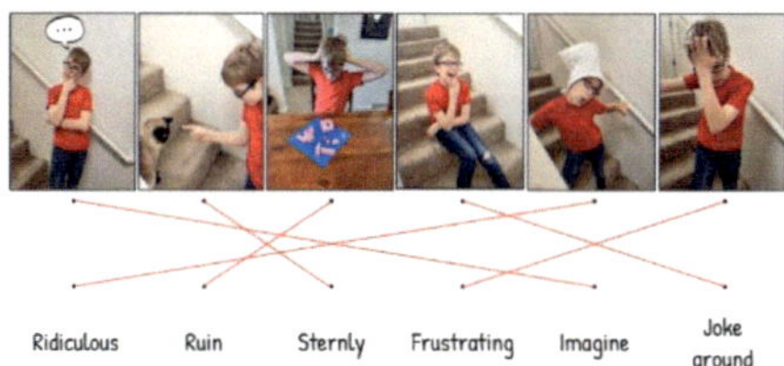

B. Circle the correct answers.

1. What does Jolly say they need?
a) a loaf of bread b) a loaf of milk c) a jug of milk

2. What does Uden say Jolly always does at school?
a) ruins everything b) runs away c) studies hard

3. How does Uden feel after Jolly says, "I'm sorry."?
a) fun b) bad c) mad

C. Read and write.

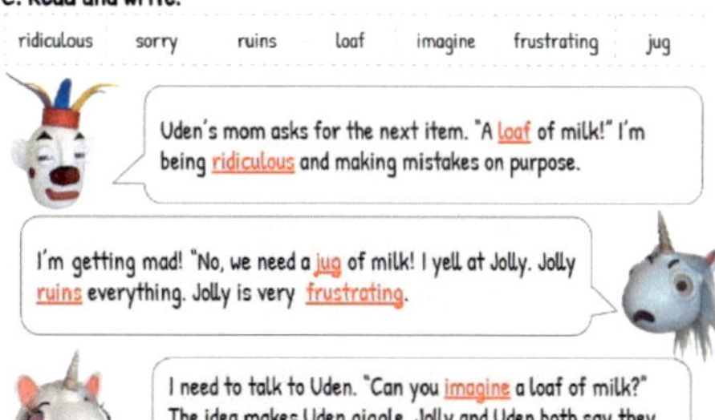

D. Circle the correct words.

1. Uden understands that working in groups can be (hard / easy).
2. Jolly would rather make jokes and (work / play) than be on task.
3. Jolly is just trying to make Uden (work / laugh).
4. It's a good idea to say you'd like to play (later / now).
5. People might joke around if they are (scared / nervous).
6. Offer to (focus / help) them instead of playing.

Activities (AK) (for pages 30-35)

A. Look and match.

Jolly says...
Uden says...
Jelly
Rice
Milk
Cereal
Ketchup
Bread

B. Circle the correct words.

1. Jolly hands the (shopping list / shopping cart) to Uden.
2. Uden surprised Mom and Jolly when he (plays along / laughs out loud) with them.
3. Mom helps Uden and Jolly choose a healthy (bag of eggs / box of cereal).
4. Uden thinks, "yuck!" because (jar of flowers / a box of ketchup) would leak.
5. Uden puts a (glass bottle / paper bag) of ketchup in the cart.
6. Jolly makes Uden laugh when he says that they need a (carton of bread / carton of eggs).

C. Read and write.

plays along with them | bread next | of ketchup in the cart | healthy box of cereal | a box of ketchup would leak | hands the shopping list to Uden

Jolly 1. hands the shopping list to Uden. Uden surprised Mom and Jolly when he 2. plays along with them. Mom helps Uden and Jolly choose a 3. healthy box of cereal. Uden thinks, "yuck!" because 4. a box of ketchup would leak though the box. Uden puts a glass bottle 5. of ketchup in the cart. Uden reads the next item on the list. They need 6. bread next. Jolly makes Uden laugh when he says that they need a carton of bread.

D. Write the sentences in the correct order.

1. (change. / Uden / doesn't like / really)
Uden really doesn't like change.

2. (is a great / become friends. / Trying / new things with / way to / people)
Trying new things with people is a great way to become friends.

3. (your own / It's / to do / way. / good to want / things)
It's good to want to do things your own way.

4. (to experience / another perspective. / allows you / things / Flexibility / from)
Flexibility allows you to experience things from another perspective.

Activities (AK) (for pages 38-43)

A. Choose and write.

1. Meg and I took the groceries out of the car.
2. There as a large owl on top of the light pole.
3. She doesn't really like to have peas with dinner.
4. Dave can eat a whole pizza by himself.
5. Oh no! The cookies got crushed by the heavy watermelon.

B. Circle true (T) or false (F).

1. They decide to get a loaf of milk. (T / **F**)
2. The groceries are on top of the bread. (T / **F**)
3. Jolly says that they should get a jug of peas. (**T** / F)
4. Mom doesn't think they can eat a whole jug of peas. (**T** / F)
5. A can of peas is delicate. (T / **F**)
6. Eggs come in a bag. (T / **F**)
7. Mom places the eggs carefully in the cart. (**T** / F)
8. The eggs get crushed. (T / **F**)

C. Read and write.

playfully delicate crushed carefully container groceries

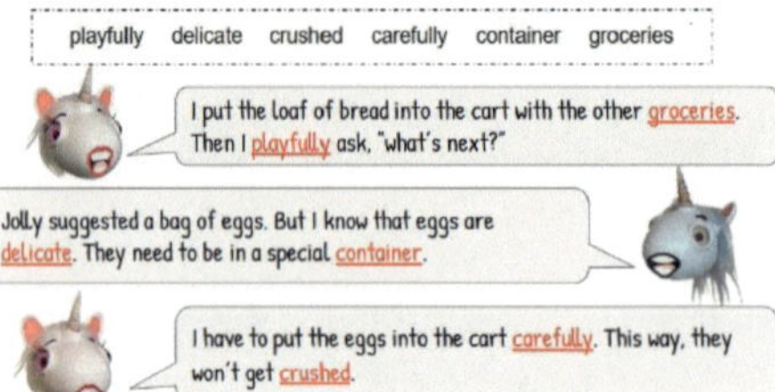

D. Choose and write.

convince choose misbehaving adult nothing

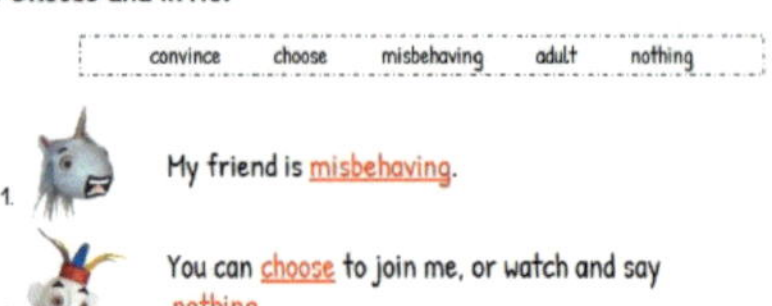

3. Or, I can tell an adult. I might try to convince Jolly to change the way he is behaving.

Activities (AK) (for pages 46-51)

A. Choose and write.

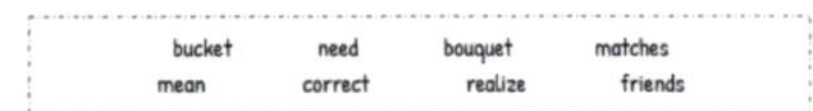

1. The color of the sky matches her eyes.
2. She had to correct the mistake she made.
3. We don't really need any more pets.
4. The boys are good friends now.
5. He gave the horse a bucket of water to drink.
6. What I mean is, I will be a little late.
7. Dad gave Mom a bouquet of flowers.
8. They didn't realize that it had started to rain.

B. Who says this? Read and match.

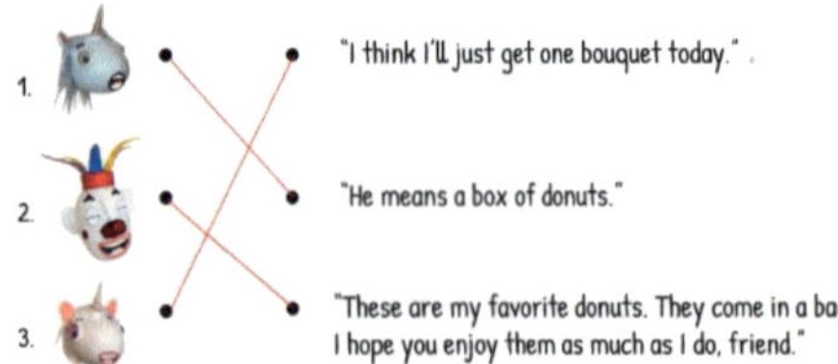

C. Choose and write.

bucket donuts nope bouquet purple corrects

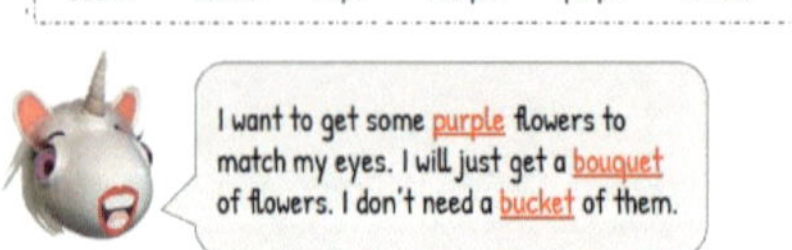

It's time for donuts! When I say we need a bag of donuts, Uden corrects me. But I say, "Nope!" because the donuts really do come in a bag, not a box.

D. Circle the correct words.

1. Sharing food helps us (realize / **bond**) with the people around us.
2. Not everyone eats the same (**food** / flowers).
3. Each family's meals are (playful / **unique**).
4. Your mom's (flower / **enchilada**) casserole might be a unique food for your family.
5. Consider the (**special** / careful) things your friends like.
6. (**Sharing** / Needing) a meal with friends can bring us closer.

Fun and Games (AK)

SECRET MESSAGE SCRAMBLE

Unscramble the words and write them in the boxes. Use the clues if needed.

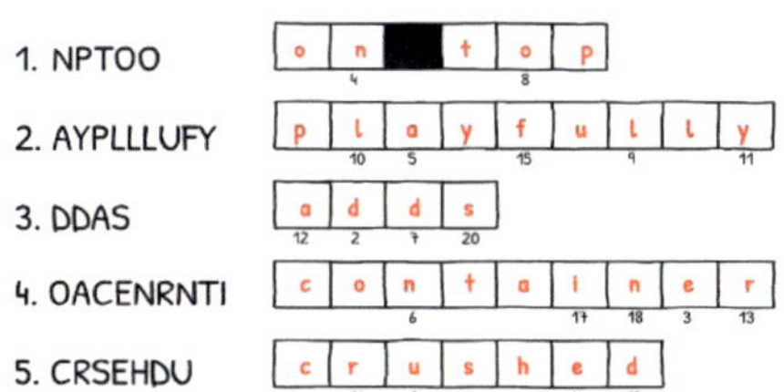

1. Uden puts a cherry on top of his ice cream sundae.
2. Jolly playfully tells jokes, but Uden doesn't think they're fun.
3. Mom adds chocolate chips to the cookie dough.
4. A jug is the typical container for milk.
5. We crushed the tomatoes to make them into spaghetti sauce.

Use the numbers from above to get a special message about Uden.

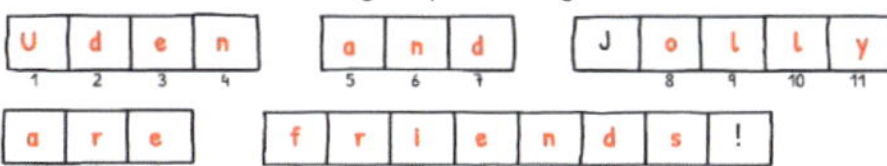

Wordsearch

Find the words in the box below hidden amoung the letters.

store	shopping list	jokes
frowns	ridiculous	imagine
healthy	bread	playfully
delicate	bucket	playdate

		e	f	s	n	b	p	s	o	r
		j	i	r	t	i	e	h	c	i
		o	d	s	o	o	s	o	k	t
		k	e	h	e	b	r	e	a	d
l	s	e	l	o	l	a	y	e	y	p
o	a	s	c	p	b	i	w	l	d	p
u	f	e	i	p	u	l	p	t	a	m
c	r	i	d	i	c	u	l	o	u	s
t	o	i	i	n	k	f	a	y	n	g
h	w	n	s	g	e	d	y	a	i	d
y	n	g	l	l	t	a	f	r	m	e
l	s	t	o	i	y	k	u	j	a	l
a	u	c	k	s	f	t	l	o	g	i
h	e	a	l	t	h	y	l	e	i	c
p	l	a	y	f	b	u	y	h	n	a
y	l	p	l	a	y	d	a	t	e	t
t	s	a	d	m	u	a	r	l	l	e

Glossary

Glossary

add [verb] to include or bring in

Let's **add** drinks to our order.

always [adverb] at all times

I **always** drink water.

announce [verb] to make known

She will **announce** when the store is open.

bag [noun] a flexible container used for holding things

Put your things in this **bag**.

bond [verb] to connect and relate with others

Eating dinner together helps my family **bond**.

boisterous [adjective] very loud, in a fun or silly way

The **boisterous** teacher was popular with his students.

bottle [noun] a narrow container without a handle used for holding liquids

Let's share a **bottle** of soda.

Glossary

bouquet [noun] several flowers that are combined together

He gave her a **bouquet** of flowers.

box [noun] a solid container that is usually square or rectangular in shape with or without a lid

We put our toys in the **box**.

bread [noun] a baked food that can be sliced and used for sandwiches

I have **bread** and butter for breakfast.

bucket [noun] a rounded container that can hold liquid or solid items

They fetch a **bucket** of water.

calorie [noun] an amount of food that helps give energy when the food is eaten

Know how many **calories** you should eat each day.

can [noun] a small, rounded container for food items that is sealed

The dog food is in a **can**.

carefully [adverb] done with care or caution

I colored the picture **carefully**.

Glossary

cart [noun] a kind of vehicle used to carry items people want to buy at a store

Our **cart** was full of food for the holiday.

carton [noun] a kind of container usually made of cardboard or other firm paper

We drink milk from a **carton** .

casserole [noun] a kid of food that is mixed and cooked in a dish

You can make a **casserole** and cook it later.

considerate [adjective] showing kindness and awareness of others

My aunt is very **considerate** .

container [noun] something used to hold or keep different items of the same kind

I need a **container** for my pencils.

convince [verb] to get someone to agree with the other

Convince me that I should give you money.

Glossary

correct [verb] to make right

Let's **correct** our mistakes and make things better.

crush [verb] to squeeze in a way that could break or destroy

Crush the strawberries to make the jam.

delicate [adjective] easily damaged

Carry the delicate flowers carefully.

donut [noun] a sweet ring-shaped breakfast or dessert food

Let's get a **donut** after the movie.

enchilada [noun] a kind of Mexican dish made with tortillas, meat, and chiles

The **enchilada** was spicy and delicious.

enjoy [verb] to like or find pleasure in something

I **enjoy** being with you.

favorite [adjective] liked more than any other

This is my **favorite** place to hike.

flexibility [noun] the ability and willingness to adjust how one thinks or behaves

When seeking your first job, **flexibility** is important.

Glossary

focus [verb] to concentrate

A quiet space helps me **focus** .

friend [noun] a person with whom another likes to spend time and have fun

My **friend** and I are going fishing.

frown [verb] to show unhappiness by turning down the corners of the mouth

She had a big **frown** after dropping her ice cream.

frustrating [adjective] causing feelings of anger and annoyance

It's **frustrating** to wait.

glass [noun] a hard, usually clear material

Don't drop the **glass** table.

groceries [noun] food items that are purchased from a store

We try to buy healthy **groceries** .

guest [noun] someone who visits another's home

Behave well when you are a **guest** .

guide [verb] to lead or direct the way

Please **guide** the way to the bathroom.

Glossary

hand [verb] to give to another person using the hands

Please **hand** this note to Beth.

healthy [adjective] benefiting the function of the body

I prefer to eat a **healthy** snack.

imagine [verb] to think about in a creative way

I can **imagine** a new world.

item [noun] an object or thing

What **item** lies behind the secret door?

jar [noun] a bottle with an opening as wide as the body

A **jar** can be hard to open.

jelly [noun] a food made from fruit that can be easily spread

I love toast and **jelly** for a snack.

joke around [idiom] to act in a fun or silly way

I like to **joke around** with my brothers.

joke [noun] something that is said or done in order to make others laugh

It's good to learn a few good **jokes**.

Glossary

jug [noun] a large container with a small opening and a handle

The **jug** is full of apple cider.

leak [verb] to pour from a small opening, usually by mistake

The boat is starting to **leak**.

loaf [noun] a shaped or molded food item such as bread or meat

We made a fresh **loaf** of bread.

match [verb] to be similar in appearance

Let's **match** our socks.

mean [verb] to intend in a specific way

Did you **mean** to bump into him?

mind [noun] the part of us that thinks, reasons, and feels

What is on your **mind**?

misbehave [verb] to behave in a negative way

Don't **misbehave** at Grandma's house.

need [verb] to be necessary or wanted

I **need** a drink of water.

Glossary

next [adverb] immediately following the previous thing

Let's visit the lion exhibit **next**.

nope [adverb] no

Nope! Not doing it.

on top of [prep. of place] at the highest point or position

On top of the building is a beautiful garden.

participate [verb] to take part in an event or activity

Would you like to **participate** in the pie-eating contest?

partner [noun] someone with whom another works on a project

We will work with a **partner** in class

peas [noun] small green vegetables from the legume family, often in cans or fresh

He mixed **peas** into his mashed potatoes.

perspective [noun] one's ideas or the facts they understand to be true

Try to see things from another's **perspective**.

play along [phrasal verb] to agree to do or accept what another person wants

When she tells you something, just **play along**.

Glossary

playfully [adverb] done is a fun or silly way

He teased her **playfully** .

polite [adjective] showing good manners toward others

Polite manners are important at the restaurant.

prefer [verb] to like more than another

I **prefer** tea over coffee.

rare [adjective] unique; not done often

It is a **rare** occasion to have the whole family together.

realize [verb] to suddenly know or understand

Do you **realize** how long this took?

reserved [adjective] calm and oftentimes quiet in personality

He is very **reserved** and prefers to watch than participate.

resist [verb] to refuse to do or act in a certain way

My dog will **resist** getting a bath.

Glossary

rice [noun] a kind of seed taken from a plant that is used in a wide assortment of cooking

We enjoy **rice** with our meals.

ridiculous [adjective] extremely silly or unreasonable

Your **ridiculous** plan will never work.

ruin [verb] to destroy

Too much water will **ruin** your garden.

shopping list [noun] a list of items needed from the store

Don't buy anything that isn't on the **shopping** list.

snack [noun] a small meal or treat

Fruit makes a great **snack**.

sorry [adjective] feeling regret over something

I'm **sorry** that I couldn't make it to your party.

sternly [adverb] showing great displeasure

He spoke **sternly** when his son ran toward traffic.

Glossary

store [noun] a place where you can buy things like food

This **store** sells items for horses.

uncomfortable [adjective] feeling distress, pain, or irritation

I am **uncomfortable** going to the party alone.

whole [adjective] all of something

Did you eat the **whole** pizza?

yuck [interjection] used to show disgust

Yuck! What's that smell?

We're glad you enjoyed Uden Unicorn!

Please share Uden with others when you're done with this book. Consider gifting this book to a younger friend or leaving it in a free Little Library.

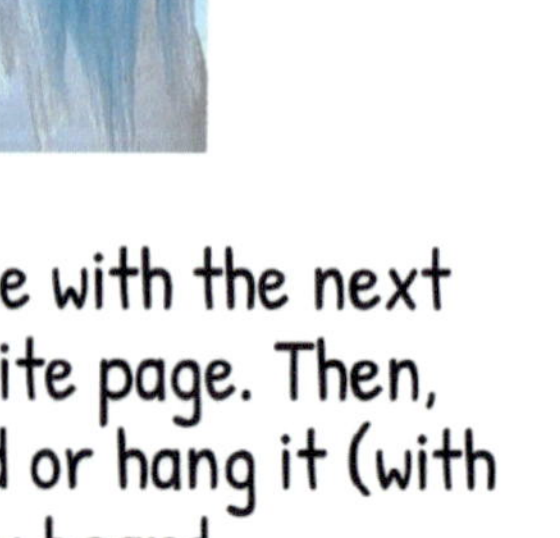

Share Uden with more people with the next few pages. Color your favorite page. Then, give your picture to a friend or hang it (with permission) on a community board.

Uden Unicorn

Uden Unicorn

Uden Unicorn

Uden Unicorn
Sparkle

Made in the USA
Columbia, SC
04 November 2024